RAINBOWS
After Storms

A Journey through Miracle, Loss, and Hope

All rights reserved. Copyright © 2023 by Dorothy Ekem A. All rights reserved. No part of this book may be reproduced, stored in a retrieval system, or transmitted by any means, electronic, mechanical, photocopying, recording, or otherwise, without written permission from the author.

ACKNOWLEDGMENT

"To my loving family, who have always believed in me and encouraged my passion for writing this book. Your unwavering support and constant presence in my life have been the driving force behind this book. To Winston and Kriston thank you for being my rock and for all the inspiration. This book is dedicated to each and every one of you, with all my love and gratitude."

I am immensely grateful for my friends and church community for their encouragement and support during the challenging moment.

Above all the one true God who carried me in situations where walking became difficult.

And to Pastor TC Bradley whose encounter made it all possible.

CONTENTS

Introduction 1

Chapter 1 3

    "The Silent Struggle: Beginning the Journey to Parenthood 3

Chapter 2 6

    You Can't Be Prepared Enough – 6

    The Discovery 8

Chapter 3 9

    Faith Season 9

    Faith at Work 10

Chapter 4 13

    Challenges Along the Way 13

Chapter 5 17

    Making A New Move 17

    First Glimmer of Hope: The Miracle Conception 18

Chapter 6 20

    Another Surprise Miracle with Joyful Moments 20

Chapter 7 22

    A Moment of Misery and Pain 22

Chapter 8 28

    Picking up the Pieces 28

Chapter 9 32

    Making The Most of My Life in Spite Of 32

    Getting Treatment 32

Chapter 10 37

    My Rainbow Baby 37

Chapter 11 45

    The Ensuing Years and My Quest to Find Atira 45

Chapter 12 48

    Big Breakthrough for Atira 48

Chapter 13 50

    Counting On with Gratitude 50

    Life Reflection 50

    Lessons Learned Along the Way 53

    There Will Always Be a Genesis and a Revelation. 58

About the Author 60

INTRODUCTION

Reproductive health issues associated with women present or manifest in various forms. The inability to conceive and give birth to offspring often occurs earlier in marriage and sometimes after having a child. Often women faced with infertility or fertility issues are adamant and hesitant to talk openly about their challenges. It's even more difficult to openly talk about loss in the event of miscarriages or stillbirths. These are moments in a woman's life where she may be burdened by guilt due to losing a would-be child, or children, and may often be attributed to the fact that she might have done something that contributed to the loss.

The guilt and burden of the loss are magnified when a woman realizes she has been stripped of the joy of motherhood. It's saddening that the initial joy of discovering being pregnant and sharing this joyful news with friends and loved ones is suddenly interrupted with an abrupt end because of the unexpected loss of the child or children.

It's such a gut-wrenching and devastating situation where women feel like the rug has been pulled right from under their feet by a tumultuous and crashing defeat filled with extreme pain and loss.

With such devastation comes an arduous road ahead of excruciating grief and loss. Thus, women going through such grief may go through episodes of denial and isolation, anger, depression, and a whirlwind of emotions.

In bereavement, many women spend different lengths of time working through the different range of emotions and express their emotions with different intensity levels. Women go through an emotional roller coaster before achieving a peaceful acceptance of the loss.

Upon going through such grief and loss, most women find it extremely hard to make room to mourn appropriately. Many of us are not afforded the luxury of time that is needed to achieve this acceptance phase after grieving a loss; only God knows how well that will end.

In my infertility journey, I've been overcome with grief and pain, followed by redemption to motherhood and success in life. Through this book, I seek to share my back-to-back losses and provide readers with a road map to grieving and ultimately reaching a place of peace and rest by overcoming their worst obstacles. In light of all my personal challenges, I have been able to live a successful and fulfilling life which has allowed me to now help others who are going through the same thing. Loss can be life-changing, it definitely changed my perspective and made me view life through a different lens. As Napoleon Hill once said, "In every adversity lies a seed of an equal or greater opportunity", so there is always a success story after adversity.

> **After a storm comes the rainbow**

CHAPTER

1

"The Silent Struggle: Beginning the Journey to Parenthood"

Subtitle: Navigating through the Challenges of Infertility

In October 1999, my world turned upside down when my OB-GYN broke the devastating news to me: my fallopian tubes were blocked. Not only that, but I had multiple fibroids, with one that had grown to the size of a five-month fetus. It felt like a nightmare unfolding before my eyes, a struggle between hope and despair battling within me.

The doctor's advised plan of action was surgery to remove the fibroids. My heart raced as I considered my dwindling options. I was cornered into making a life-altering decision, and the weight of it pressed heavily on my chest. It was either undergo the daunting procedure or face the harsh reality that conceiving a child might remain an unattainable dream for me.

The surgery loomed over me like a dark cloud. We are talking about a major surgery with the healing process estimated to be between 4 to 6 weeks. My options were undeniably slim. On one hand, there was the possibility of overcoming this hurdle, and on the other, a future of coming to terms with the incapability to conceive.

The turmoil within me was indescribable. My lifelong wish to experience motherhood now vehemently clashed with the threat of a potential surgery which presented me with feelings of fear and uncertainty. So many questions swirled through my mind, painting my thoughts with anxiety and dread. Was this my only chance at motherhood? Were the risks worth it? Was there any guarantee that the surgery would pave the way for a child?

I returned home and delved deeply into researching fibroids. The more I discovered, the greater my apprehension grew. It's fair to say that the internet might not always be the most reassuring place to seek answers, especially after receiving unsettling news. Yet here I was seeking clarity online. Although I was in the midst of overwhelming information and many speculative questions, I stumbled upon a few articles that offered a glimmer of hope.

My life-long desire to be a mother has festered for as long as I can remember, from my adolescence to adulthood. Now, I found myself at a crossroads where this deep-seated desire seems unattainable and almost impossible. At this point I quickly decided to take up my report up in prayer to the Almighty physician—God. He's the only one who knows all our struggles, but still give a better report that is contrary to the physician's report.

The journey before me was undoubtedly one brimming with hurdles, embodying every conceivable season. It resembled traversing through the climatic seasons of existence, and encountering mountains, hills, valleys, clear, sunny days, rainy days, and tempestuous times, just to name a few.

Truthfully, there were numerous instances where I yearned to bypass such seasons if given a choice, but life unfolded contrary to my preferences. That's the essence of existence. Circumstances do not always align with individual yearnings or needs. Certain predicaments surpass our realm of influence, but our reactions to life's predicaments remain within our domain.

Gazing through the lenses of optimism enables us to react positively to every favorable or unfavorable circumstance, maximizing every situation to yield optimum results.

CHAPTER

2

You Can't be Prepared Enough –

We were a young couple starting life in New Jersey. I call this season summer because I was comfortable and excited about the future. During this season, I was getting myself acclimatized to my new married life and the dream of raising a beautiful family. Yet this hope dissipated when I received the bad news about my health.

My doctor's report came as a shock and a surprise. I never imagined for one second that getting pregnant would become a challenge. This became a devastating reality for me that couldn't wrap my mind around. Little did I know that I would be living with the reality of facing infertility issues.

Growing up I always loved little kids and I was so fond of my neighbor kids. Children give me a special kind of joy. It was a deep desire that had festered for so long in my heart.

> "Delight yourself in the LORD, and he will give you the desires of your heart."
> Psalm 37:4

I knew I would need a miracle, which might take some time with this one, so I prayed this prayer. It went like this: "Dear God, you know I love children and can't see myself without having them. I understand it might take some time, but I don't want to wait for years, I am trusting you for a miracle. Amen". Why did I say years? Well, I knew a lady at my church who had been waiting for seven years, and we have been praying for her. After my prayer, I felt peace over me and decided not to share the news with anyone, but rather start believing for my miracle.

A little back story for this faith of mine. A few years prior to this news, I accepted Christ and became a born-again Christian. My personal relationship with Christ gave me a deeper meaning of life and the opportunity to experience firsthand the grace and favor of God. He opened several doors and overwhelmed me with so many blessings. You know that kind of blessing that you can't claim the glory but literally attribute all of it to God? Yes...that's the kind of blessing I am talking about. I believe this walk with anyone Him prepared me for the news. If you are reading this and you are not a born-again believer, I know you will probably have doubts or unbelief, but hear me out. I have had those moments too. There were times I struggled to understand the challenges I was about to go through. The truth is no one can be prepared enough for this news.

The Discovery

What led me to discover my fertility issue? Well, my co-worker started a conversation about her trip to the gynecologist and her startling discovery of her infertility issues. They had put off having kids for years, but the minute they decided to have kids, they had this setback. At the end of the conversation, she advised me to check up with my gynecologist and avoid what she had discovered. I took her advice and made my first appointment with a doctor.

My first appointment with the gynecologist was routine. After a couple of visits, he agreed to run some lab tests. Although my blood work was fine, my gynecologist discovered I had multiple fibroids, the largest of which was about the size of a five-month-old fetus. He was concerned about the findings and requested that I do a hysterosalpingogram (HSG), which is a diagnostic procedure to view the inside of the uterus and fallopian tubes.

What was even more surprising and shocking was that the procedure revealed that my fallopian tubes were blocked. I learned from my gynecologist for the very first time about the unlikelihood of me getting pregnant. This new realization hit me to the core, and I couldn't bring myself to accept that I would not have any children. This news rocked my boat with a whirlwind of emotions and unanswered questions. I never anticipated these results, but I was glad I took my friend's advice which led to my discovery....and the question remains.... what's next?

CHAPTER

3

Faith Season

Upon receiving the medical report from my gynecologist, I found myself deluged by a whirlwind of thoughts, each trying to paint potential future scenarios. Although questions like "What if?" and "How will I deal with this?" swirled around in my head, I chose to embark on a journey of faith, with hoping of finding a pathway to the miracle of motherhood. While the doctor's diagnosis stemmed from their expertise based on test that indicate the presence of fibroids, I drew strength from Isaiah 53:5, which says, "By His stripes, I am healed and made whole." placed my trust in the unwavering divinity of God, believing in His Divine insight regarding my situation. The doctors provided facts, but I know God holds the ultimate truth about my destiny. After all, nothing is impossible with God, as stated in Matthew 19:26.

Faith at Work

In spite of the flood of bad news about my infertility issues, I was determined to be hopeful, stay afloat, and not drown in negativity. By applying the word of God in the Bible to my situation, I boldly confessed that it is possible for me to attain motherhood. I surrendered all my burdens, cares, and worries to God by praying and handing over the medical report to Him to take over. For it is written that we should cast all our burdens and cares upon Him, and He will give us rest...Matthew 11:28. In communicating my cares and worries to God through prayer, I affirmed my trust in Him alone to help me. In my prayer, I said, 'I don't know how, and I don't know when, but you, my God, got this'. Indeed, there is nothing too difficult for You, God, to do....... Jeremiah 32:17, Genesis 18:14. If you are reading and you are not a believer, you will probably say, "I am not a Christian or not even religious." I would say, "No problem." neither was the woman with the issue of blood; she still received her healing. All she had was her persistent in pursuit of Jesus and her belief that if she could touch him, she would be healed. In addition to this, Jesus proclaimed, "Healing is the children's bread" (Matthew 15:26), affirming that healing is accessible to all. Our ignorance of this fact does not negate its validity.

During my season of faith, I sought out individuals who had endured similar trials like mine, and hoped their stories would strengthen my own faith and belief. It wasn't hard to find these individuals. Many had astonishing faith challenging circumstances like mine.

However, one woman, in particular, stood out to me—her steadfast faith left a profound impression in my heart. She was a member of my church, and like me, she had been waiting on the Lord for a child. After seven years and numerous unsuccessful attempts at conception, her perseverance was remarkable. In November 1999, joyous news spread that she was expecting. The excitement grew even more when we learned that she was blessed not with one child, but with twins.

The news of this woman's pregnancy after such a prolonged period of anticipation acted as a catalyst, and ignited a renewed sense of hope and excitement within me. I looked at her story as a beacon of hope, and was encouraged that my faith could achieve a miracle. Her story allowed me to dream with a reinvigorated spirit that perhaps my own longing was not in vain, and that the dream of cradling my own child was not just a mirage, but a future reality. Her blessing became a source of inspiration, a wellspring from which I drew the courage to envision my life's next chapter as a mother.

I made a conscious choice to use her narrative as a powerful antidote to counteract any negative thoughts that threatened to cloud my vision. In the quiet corners of my prayers, I began to entrust God with my honesty, and to confess that the virtue of patience she had shown felt beyond my grasp. I didn't know how long I would be called to walk the path of waiting for this deeply personal miracle to occur. A steadfast hope, however, was firmly rooted in my heart. A quiet assurance came over me and gave me peace that it would indeed happen for me in God's perfect timing.

In those moments of vulnerability, when the silence around me seemed to echo with the emptiness, I reached out to God. With each prayer, I laid the depths of my anguish before Him, the anguish that only He could truly understand. In these intimate encounters with the divine, I found solace. I knew that within His boundless capacity to perform wonders, He held the tender power to weave the miracle of life and fulfill my deepest desire to embrace motherhood.

CHAPTER

4

CHALLENGES ALONG THE WAY

The initial notion of exposing the raw and personal truth of my infertility struggles was deeply intimidating. The thought of opening up about something so close to my heart, especially to those who might not understand or share my faith in God's plan, filled me with dread. I feared the possible reactions — the whisper of judgment in their voices, the shadow of pity in their eyes, or worse, the sting of ridicule. These potential responses loomed over me, heavy as the diagnosis itself, and I was petrified of being seen not just as childless, but as less capable or worthy in the eyes of those I cared about.

Despite these fears, as time inched forward, a quiet strength began to emerge from within me. It was time to revisit the professional who had been with me on this journey from the start, my gynecologist. So, with a heart full of hope and a mind braced for reality, I returned to his office.

In the sterile but safe confines of the doctor's office, my gynecologist presented the next steps with a blend of medical expertise and compassionate care. It was clear that before we could even begin to think about conception, we had to create a healthier environment for a potential pregnancy. The fibroids, which had become unwelcome tenants in my womb, needed to be removed.

This surgery was not just a medical procedure; it was a gateway, a necessary passage toward healing and fertility. The doctor assured me that post-surgery, we could take a fresh look at my condition with a new perspective and develop a tailored approach to treatment. The objective was to address the underlying issues causing my infertility, thereby increasing the chances of achieving a successful pregnancy.

This suggested path brought a mix of emotions, and anxiety about the operation mingled with optimism for what it represented. With each step taken on this path, I was moving closer to the possibility of motherhood, closer to the dream that had nestled itself so deeply in my soul. The journey was fraught with unknowns, but it was a journey I was willing to embark upon. It was fortified by faith and hope of what lay beyond the surgical intervention — the hope of life.

The original plan was for the surgical removal of my fibroids to take place in December of 1999, a date set by my gynecologist. However, the approach of the year's end brought with it not only the usual introspection but also the added anxiety over the widely publicized Y2K bug and its potential complications. The prospect of undergoing major surgery amid the uncertainty surrounding the millennium bug was disquieting. The very thought of the surgery chilled me to the core, and fear for my well-being was tangible. The idea of welcoming the year 2000 in recovery, bound to my bed, and battling through six weeks of convalescence, was daunting.

Driven by these concerns, I lobbied for the surgery to be postponed until January 2000. As I did, a part of me clung to the hope that the appointed day might be averted altogether. This brief postponement felt like a reprieve, a precious pause that might allow room for a miracle. During this pause, I found myself seeking solace and strength in prayer more fervently than ever before.

I petitioned for a Divine turn-around in my condition, a change so profound that it would make the looming surgery unnecessary. With each prayer, I sought not just physical healing, but also a peace of mind, and a reassurance that transcended the fears and uncertainties of my situation. My heart held onto the possibility of a miracle - one that would free me from the impending operation and ensuing pain, but also usher me into a new chapter filled with health and joy.

In a challenging period like the one I was facing, it felt nearly impossible to divert my attention to other facets of my life. The issue of my infertility seemed to loom over me, threatening to snatch away my joy and monopolize my time. I found that worry had a way of creeping in, and urging me to delve into research about my condition. This only shifted my focus back to the impending surgery, and totally consumed my thoughts.

During this time, I learned the importance of being intentional with my mindset. I had to consciously steer my thoughts away from anxiety and towards positivity. Each day became an exercise in self-encouragement. I adopted a proactive attitude, deliberately guarding against the negative thoughts that attempted to intrude my mind.

In a gesture of hope and defiance, I even began buying baby clothes and dolls, anything I felt might serve as a catalyst for my miracle. Such actions were more than just symbolic, they fostered a sense of anticipation and joy within me. I was under no illusion that there was much I could physically do to alter my circumstances, but I refused to sit in sorrow. Instead, I engaged in activities that I believed could invite divine intervention.

Despite her long wait to conceive, the woman from my church always appeared vibrant and joyful, at least outwardly. Her demeanor constantly reminded me that the essence of faith is not in succumbing to fear, but in maintaining joy and hope against all odds.

As for the surgery, the thought of a five to six-week recovery period was daunting, filling me with much trepidation. Yet, I reminded myself where faith dwells, fear should have no place to stand. It became a daily battle to hold onto my faith, and let it be the foundation upon which I stood to navigate the uncertainties and fears of my situation.

> *"He who dwells in the shelter of the Most High will abide in the shadow of the Almighty. I will say to the LORD, 'My refuge and my fortress, my God, in whom I trust.'"*
> *Psalm 91:1-2*

CHAPTER

5

Making A New Move

My husband and I were looking to relocate from our current New Jersey residence to a whole new place. Although some part of didn't want to move, yet another part of me agreed, almost as if a new location would bring a fresh perspective.

We were, however, uncertain of where we should relocate. One day while my husband searched the internet for possible locations to move to, let him to discovered the Ohio as a State choice. I wasn't totally sold on this new location, and neither were my close relatives, especially considering how far it was from New Jersey.

We finally decided to visit Ohio on Christmas Eve to explore the state. For me, church service at Christmas time was a standing tradition that I would not miss out on. So, on the Sunday before we left for Ohio, I sowed a seed at church for my upcoming surgery, since I knew we wouldn't be in New Jersey for Christmas service.

Upon arriving in Columbus, Ohio, I was pretty amazed at how peaceful the place was compared to Jersey. From what we knew of New Jersey, it was like night and day, probably because the new location in Columbus felt like a breath of fresh air from all the news about my medical issues. I found Columbus, Ohio, to be an okay place to be. During our stay, we went apartment hunting and settled on one nice apartment to move into. By early January 2000, we had to quickly wrap up our trip in Columbus and head back to New Jersey. Once in New Jersey, we had to end our lease before we could relocate to the new apartment in Ohio. Going back to New Jersey also meant having to face my upcoming surgery to remove the fibroids and to get to the bottom of my infertility issues.

"First Glimmer of Hope: The Miracle Conception"

We submitted all paperwork needed for the apartment and were given a move-in date of March 1st, 2000. Shortly after our trip came another twist and surprising turn of events. I was riding with my husband from work when someone accidentally rear-ended our vehicle. As a result of the accident, later that night I experienced some pain that caused me go to the ER to get it checked out.

At the ER they wanted to take some x-rays, so the nurse asked, I guess, the routine question, whether I was pregnant, and my answer was, "no, I don't think so". She said as a precautionary measure she would perform a pregnancy test before the x-ray. To my utmost surprise, the pregnancy test revealed that I was pregnant, and therefore could not go through with the x-ray as previously planned to check out my back pain. They discharged me with Tylenol and asked me to follow up with my OBGYN. For the rest of the night, although I was overwhelmed with joy, I was eagerly awaiting daybreak to find out if my pregnancy now meant no surgery.

I called the gynecologist in the morning to inform him, and he had his thoughts and concerns. He said it was a miracle for me to have gotten pregnant, and he ordered blood work to be done. I waited patiently for the results, and it finally came to confirm. He wanted to see me, my husband, and goodness gracious, what a tall list of all the things that could go wrong with the pregnancy! I was diagnosed with a high-risk pregnancy with the possibility of miscarriage, premature birth, cesarean section, bed rest, etc. All this he said was not to scare me but as a precaution and not to get my hopes up too high.

We finally moved to Columbus, Ohio, on March 1st, 2000. This new move meant no surgery for now.

I, however, stayed in New Jersey to be attended to by my doctor and his team for pre-natal checkups for a few months. In May 2000, I was able to join my husband in Columbus and was able to find a new team of doctors and health care professionals in our new location.

Thank God for this miracle of being able to get pregnant. I went on to have my first child, a healthy baby boy who brought so much joy to our home and family with the usual pregnancy moments. He was two days overdue and was delivered by a caesarian, as cautioned by my physician.

CHAPTER

6

Another Surprise Miracle with Joyful Moments

In July of 2001, I decided to return to school while my son was about 10 months old. In March 2002, I discovered I was pregnant with baby number two. My son was seventeen months old, I was working, and was also in school full time. I must admit that I was overwhelmed with the news. I guess I was hoping that would happen after my son's second birthday. Because I continued to work and didn't drop out of school, I had to make some mental adjustments. After a couple of months, I was able to manage and balance everything.

> It was another surprise pregnancy,

My pregnancy was progressing well. We decided around May that we needed a bigger place for our new addition, so we started house hunting. This was really exciting, but a bit stressful because of the time constraint. Since the baby was due the first week of November, so we only had six months to find a house. We were initially going for a new build that wouldn't be ready before the baby, so we settled for an existing home that was difficult to find. We also discovered that there was a high probability that we were having a baby girl. We finally found a house that was a perfect fit for what we needed; it had a room already decorated in pink and was suitable for a girl. We made an offer, which was accepted two months before delivery. We were hoping that we would close on the house and move before the baby's delivery. It seemed like everything was in order in anticipation of our new arrival. I believe I had the grace to carry my daughter. She was a very active baby, and most of the time, you could see her movement outside my belly.

> She made her presence felt in the belly out of the belly. Parents get to meet their little ones before they get introduced to the world.

Time flew by so quickly, and soon, my belly looked like I was having twins, I was huge and still working and in school. I was doing well, and my OBGYN was okay with all my activities.

My co-worker organized a surprise baby shower for me the first week in October. That weekend, my family and friends also organized a surprise shower for me, so many gift items of baby clothes, accessories, bassinettes, toys, gift cards, and money were given towards the birth of our second child. This was such a joyful time of our lives for which we were so grateful to God as a family, especially knowing that our son, who was about two years old at the time, would soon have a siblings to play with.

CHAPTER

7

A Moment of Misery and Pain

This pregnancy was truly one of a kind. The baby was active and kept me up most of the night. It felt like two kids struggling in the belly....and I can relate to Rebecca's story carrying Jacob and Esau (Genesis 25:23). Thankfully, my pregnancy had progressed successfully, and pre-natal checkups with my gynecologist resulted in excellent reports of a healthy ongoing pregnancy all this time. My schoolwork and classes were also on track with my college degree. I had finished a year in my four-year program.

> All was going well, and then the setback. Setbacks are always setups you don't see that when it's happening.

Two weeks after the joyous occasion of our baby shower, and deep into my third trimester at thirty-seven and a half weeks on October 21st, 2002, I was enveloped in a mixture of excitement and anticipation. I was scheduled for one of my regular pre-natal checkups, and expected the routine of hearing the same comforting sounds and reassurances that came with every visit.

The day gave no indication of the turmoil it would soon bring.

The week prior, I had discussed baby's movement in detail with my doctor because she was overly active. He had remarked on the baby's heart rate, which was at a steady 155. With a note of casualness, he mentioned how female babies usually exhibit a slightly higher heart rate than their male counterparts. Life was busy with more than pregnancy preparations. We were on the point of acquiring a new home and making a nest for our expanding family. Everything felt as it should. A harmonious blend of expectancy and routine.

That harmony was disrupted during the checkup. As the doctor searched for the familiar thud of the baby's heartbeat, his expression switched into one of concern. This was not the same face of the doctor I knew before, the one who always had reassuring news. He gently suggested I get dressed and meet him in his office. The sanctuary of his office, where he had shared so much positive news in the past, became the setting for the most heart-wrenching revelation: our baby's heartbeat was now silent.

Overwhelmed with disbelief and confusion, I called my husband and my aunt. The wait for a family member to show up felt like ages. At that moment, my faith, which had been a guiding light, seemed obscured by shadows of doubt. I yearned for God's reassuring touch, for a miracle to drive out the gathering darkness.

Hoping against hope, my family arrival and decided to get a second opinion. We headed to Mount Carmel Hospital, praying that they would uncover a different truth. A heartbeat resounded in the room almost immediately after an ultrasound at the hospital. For a brief, euphoric moment, it felt as though our prayers had been answered. But that excitement evaporated when we learned that it was my heartbeat echoing, not our baby's. The painful reality dawned on us: our little girl was gone.

Grief and shock overwhelmed my senses, and I felt lost in a storm of emotions, ending in a full-blown panic attack. Amidst our pain, a compassionate doctor at Mount Carmel reached out, his words and demeanor a testament to his empathy for our profound loss.

> I didn't know how I would survive this; there surely was an abundance of grace. When there is no escape from the situation you are going through, he gives you grace to carry you through it.

By the afternoon, the weight of our situation had settled in, and we were faced with a heart-wrenching decision. Our medical team advised against a prolonged delay in delivering the baby, citing potential health risks to me. The exact duration since our baby's passing remained a mystery, and every moment that passed threatened complications for my other organs. Urgency was the watchword. The doctor granted us a brief respite, suggesting we reconvene later that evening for a cesarean delivery.

We went home to get ready for the delivery. Seeing my 2-year-old son at home was comforting; however, the idea of him not meeting her sister was too much for me. I remember when his sister was super active, I would place his hand on my belly to feel the kicks, and he would ask so many questions. He was our miracle, and now I am on my knee for a turn-around moment. We collected my essentials and returned to the hospital, my heart was heavy with grief and unanswered questions. Throughout this ordeal, I reached out to the same divine presence that had once blessed me with this pregnancy. Now, consumed by sorrow and feeling abandoned, I pleaded for strength, support, and understanding, even daring to voice my questions to God amidst the silence.

I called my church for prayers and held on to my faith. Who am I to question God when he has done so much in the past? I am human, and we turn to ask questions in times like this, so I did question him but did not hear an answer. He is God in good times and bad. I still need him to pull me through the surgery.

> God gave me strength I never knew I had. In times of tribulations, he introduces us to our better self. He steps aside and allows us to discover ourselves.

They prepared me for surgery. Although it was my second time, this time was different. I couldn't go through with it because I was stricken with fear and panic. Nothing the doctors and nurses did could relax or help me go through the operation. It felt like I was going to die…. literally…. Finally, my doctor gave me full anesthesia. The baby was born at 9:40pm on October 21st, 2002, and weighed 5 pounds and was 19 inches long.

Such was the weight of pain and misery I felt that I wished I didn't have to wake up to the terrible news of such a painful loss. Well, I did wake up to pain and misery! The good news was I made it through surgery.

The next day was eventful as we were scheduled to close on our first home. The realtors couldn't reschedule our 22nd closing date, so we had to close the house at the hospital a day after losing our baby. It was a bittersweet moment. Although we closed on our first home, but the baby behind this dream couldn't make it. We got that out of the way and got back to mourning our baby.

Holding our precious baby in my arms, even if only for a short time, provided a fleeting respite from the searing pain of loss. The hospital staff, keenly aware of the depth of my anguish, took special care in dressing her in soft pink clothes, wrapping her snugly in warm blankets, and handing her to me with the utmost gentleness. This gesture, although seemingly simple, was a profound act of empathy. They allowed us to connect and bond, granting me a moment to cherish her presence amidst the overwhelming grief. The preservation of her tiny form during my hospital stay showcased their compassion, ensuring she appeared peacefully asleep.

Bestowing upon her a beautiful name Atira (Hebrew-meaning pray) felt like a tribute to the life that could have been. We allowed our family and friends to meet her, sharing our grief and offering support. The comfort I derived from holding her close was overshadowed by the knowledge that our time together was brief. Tears seemed to flow endlessly as I tried to imprint every detail of her face, every sensation of her weight in my arms, into my memory. The hospital staff, recognizing the depths of my sorrow, provided the needed space to grieve, and always approached us with extreme sensitivity, especially whenever the inevitable discussions about her final resting place arose.

With the hospital's suggestion of a private burial, the weight of making another painful decision pressed down on us. Our grief, already all-consuming, rendered us unable to navigate the intricacies of organizing a burial. In a desperate bid for some solace, we entrusted the hospital with the responsibility of cremating and burying our precious baby girl.

As if the emotional torment wasn't enough, I found myself grappling with excruciating physical pain, an unwelcomed aftermath of the delivery. The spinal anesthesia, which had been administered during labor, had unintended repercussions, leading to near-paralyzing neck pain which resulted in a spinal headache. To alleviate the discomfort, my doctor suggested a blood patch treatment. Unfortunately, this brought no relief. Feeling defeated and lonely, I was sent home with mere painkillers. But life, however in its mysterious ways, sometimes provides solutions in the unlikeliest of places. A revelation about caffeine's potential relief led me to a bottle of Mountain Dew. That familiar, simple drink became an unexpected savior that helped to ease the physical pain and offer a small trace of normalcy in the storm of my emotions.

CHAPTER

8

Picking up the Pieces

Upon arriving home after being discharged from the hospital, we had a good support system, which included family and friends, as well as our church family. They were able to help us put together a nice memorial service for our baby girl. My pastor's wife sent us a beautiful flower basket with a handwritten note. Later, we found out that she had gone through a similar loss.

Tears and a roller coaster of emotions which almost seemed like an unending whirlwind. I think our body changes with the expectation of a new baby coming. The tidal wave of emotion, from the anticipation of becoming a mother to the heartache of loss, were relentless. It felt as if I was aboard a roller coaster that refused to stop, each twist and turn echoing the highs and lows of my experience. With every crest of joy came a trough of sorrow - the two intertwined in a dance that left me breathless and overwhelmed.

The physical metamorphosis reminded me of the life that blossomed within me. Every kick and every flutter I felt during the pregnancy had painted vivid images of a future filled with baby giggles, first steps, and tender moments. But with the passing of our baby girl, these once-joyful reminders now felt like echoes in an empty hall, reverberating with the weight of what could have been.

As my body began to adjust to the changes, the swell of my belly, the tenderness of my breasts, and the myriad other shifts that come with expecting a baby, became a living testament to the life that had been promised but was now lost. These physical changes, which once signaled the joyous arrival of a new family member, now served as a bittersweet reminder of the dreams and hopes I once nurtured.

It's a peculiar paradox — to feel your body prepare and change in anticipation of a new life but then have to grapple with the void left behind. This contrast of life's most profound joys and deepest sorrows is a testament to the resilience of the human spirit and the depth of a mother's love. Through the storm of emotions and the ever-present reminders etched into my very being, I found strength I never knew I had. navigating the complexities of grief, love, and healing.

> Today, there are lots of social media groups that help with grieving parents. Back then, organizations like "A Stitch In Time made my daughter's outfit and gave me materials to help me heal.

Thankfully, with the help of family, friends, and my church family, I was given emotional, spiritual, and social support. There were frequent visits, times of fellowship, and prayer that not only gave me hope, but also encouragement that built my faith in God to continue to live my life again and do the things that I loved to do.

The circle of support around me, and my faith in God helped me to the greatest extent possible by breaking me out of the rut of seemingly insurmountable pain and misery, as well as the unending emotional whirlwind that I couldn't have overcome single-handedly.

> "'For I know the plans I have for you,' declares the Lord, 'plans to prosper you and not to harm you, plans to give you a hope and a future.'" — Jeremiah 29:11
> This bible verse was me.

I was aware of God's love and promises but needed a bible quote to affirm His promises. As apostle Paul said in Philippians 3:13-14, "forgetting the past and pressing on toward the goal to win the prize for which God has called me heavenward in Christ Jesus". As a way of trying to totally blot out the memory of the devastating loss of my baby, I kept all the baby shower gifts for my daughter tucked away in the attic of the house. By keeping all the baby gift items completely out of my sight helped not to serve as a constant reminder of my painful loss. Although each time I passed by what would have been her room, the pink walls and art decorations reminded me of her.

Another way I managed to find consolation and encouragement was through my son. The thought of knowing that in spite of the loss of my daughter, my son was still here with me. I was aware of the fact I still had him, although he wasn't old enough to experience the loss.

> Isaiah 55:8-11. God is saying.
> "For as the heavens are higher than the earth, so are my ways higher than your ways, and my thoughts than your thoughts."

CHAPTER

9

MAKING THE MOST OF MY LIFE IN SPITE OF

Getting Treatment

The autopsy results were unveiled, revealing an unexpected and unfamiliar term as the cause of death: hyper-coiling of the umbilical cord. As I grappled with this term and its implications, a tidal wave of emotions crashed over me, primarily frustration and confusion. Why hadn't my doctor proposed an early stress test, especially given my history of a previous high-risk pregnancy? It felt as if additional preventive measures should have been an obvious course of action.

Determined to understand, I plunged into deep research, sifting through medical journals and articles to discern if this tragic and heart-wrenching outcome might have been averted. My grief and need for answers pushed me towards considering legal action. Multiple consultations with attorneys followed, many of whom believed that there was a legitimate case to pursue.

But as the days turned to weeks, reflection made me realize that my drive towards legal action was more a manifestation of my pain and grief than a quest for justice. The thought of courtrooms and legal battles, while initially seemed like a path to closure, began to feel like another layer of torment. I needed to focus on the present and on the healing process, not only for myself, but also for the sake of my son.

Making the decision to switch doctors was not easy. Still, it was a step towards gaining some semblance of control in a situation where I felt so powerless. As time continued its relentless march forward, I embarked on a journey of forgiveness. Despite his perceived oversight, my former doctor was human. I recognized that holding onto bitterness and anger would not change the past. It could, however, jeopardize my future well-being and happiness.

Forgiving doesn't always come easy. It's a complex process that requires time, reflection, and, often, a deep spiritual connection. I chose to release my resentment and allowed myself to trust in a greater plan and purpose, guided by a higher power. It was a challenging path, filled with introspection and emotional turmoil. Still, it became a crucial part of my healing journey. Life goes on no matter what, but the thought of getting pregnant again was terrifying to the extent that I didn't want to have any more kids. We went to see my new doctor about this, however we weren't aligned with the options to use a 5-year intrauterine device (IUD) as a way of contraception, so I settled for a patch.

He advised me to take this time to address the fibroid, so I did and finally had the surgery to remove the fibroids. I had a myomectomy, which a less invasive surgery to remove the smaller fibroids. Unfortunately, this did not unblock my left fallopian tube, and the results were very short-lived. Soon after the surgery the fibroids came back again, and my doctor started a discussion of doing something more invasive.

After a year, we decided to try again, but this time, I wasn't getting pregnant. My doctor referred me to a fertility specialist after a few trials with clomid, which is a medication that is used to treat infertility in women. We sought out infertility treatment and hoped to have a successful pregnancy.

After we went through all the blood work and screening, and our first try was successful.

Although my third pregnancy was a success, sadly just about twelve weeks after becoming pregnant, I suffered a medical emergency of excruciating pain in my abdomen, so we called 911. Upon arriving at the hospital, they paged my doctor, who quickly rushed in. After being examined by my gynecologist, I was found to have experienced an ectopic pregnancy, which resulted in rupturing my fallopian tubes. Since my blood pressure was very low, the doctor called for an emergency surgery to remove the baby. Because this affected my blocked tube, the rapture had caused me to lose a lot of blood. During surgery it became apparent that the tube's damage was life-threatening so they had to remove the left fallopian tubes. My gynecologist was, however, quick to emphasize that thankfully the immediate rush to get me to the hospital saved my life. It we had waited another thirty minutes, then I possibly could have lost my life.

The loss came as another blow to my path to motherhood. On my way to surgery this time, my husband said, "I think this is it, we're blessed with one child, and we should be happy to have him", and I couldn't have agreed more. Thankfully, I came out of surgery not needing a blood transfusion, but I was still very weak due to the loss of blood. I managed to put this loss behind me. Sometimes things happen that we have no control over, yet we keep trusting God, and we keep believing in His word. Why wasn't this pregnancy successful? I couldn't tell, but this I know: He is the same yesterday, today, and forever. Every pregnancy and every child is different. Although they may all come from the same belly, they however, don't have the same destiny. These pregnancies were teaching me something, but it was too painful to learn during the process. Someone may ask what can possibly be learned from this process, except pain and agony. For me, it made me a stronger person, after experiencing one loss after another. When this happens, you begin to see everyone around you who is having a baby, and you ask yourself why you keep losing yours.

For some people, pregnancy loss means no longer going to baby showers, or seeing pregnant women because it reminds them of their loss. That happened to me with my first loss. While in the hospital, a lady who had suffered a similar loss was sent to talk to me. Still, I resented this and told her I wasn't interested in her story. Later that day, I thought about my actions towards her and felt really bad about it. A loud voice inside of me said, "This is not who you are." I asked if I could speak to the lady again, but she had been discharged. From that point on in the hospital, I decided that I wasn't going to let my loss cause me to resent those carrying successful pregnancies and baby showers. I thank God for that revelation. Although I wasn't nice to the lady in the hospital, it, however, showed me that this could cause me to become an ugly person on the inside if I didn't change my perspective. I love pregnancy, and I believe pregnant women are some of the most beautiful women. I started to realize that if I didn't change, I would now be allowing my loss to cause me to resent something that I have always loved. The question now becomes an oxymoron, how can you love something that you now resent. Some women start off with loving to be pregnant, and then pregnancy loss causes them to now resent the very thing they once desired. This is where I claim that this back-to-back loss made me stronger, because I had to now live it every day, and also confess my positive outlook on pregnancy. I helped my friend with baby showers and helped a close relative through a difficult pregnancy. I know very well that the devil comes but to steal, kill, and destroy. Still, the son of God came that I may have life and life more abundantly (John 10:10). I learned to never give up on my dream, and with prayers and supplication, I made my request known to God.

CHAPTER

10

My Rainbow Baby

In 2005, we decided to try again, so we went through another fertility treatment. This time, it required more testing each month. The one thing I dreaded the most was the shots. I can't stand needles, so daily shots were my nightmare. One day it occurred to me that I could freeze my thigh and not feel the poking of the needle, so I got an ice pack and laid it on my thigh till it was numb. It worked! From that day on, I never had any problem with my daily shot. This definitely was a learning curve, which is why I said this experience taught me a lot. Patience was one of the lessons learned, and boy, I am still learning this. I met women during this journey who were on their second, third, and fourth attempts, who still had not given up, which gave me the courage to also not to give up. Children are truly gifts from God, and as much as we pray and ask for these precious gifts, we should also follow the guidance of our doctors when seeking fertility treatment.

A medical report is not always the final report, as I experienced at the beginning of my story, because our God can do exceedingly abundantly above all that we can ask or think (Ephesians 3:20).

The treatment went well, and for the second time, I became pregnant again. It took great grace, as the scripture says in 2 Corinthians 9:8, "And God is able to make all grace abound to you". This time, we weren't going to share the news until after the first trimester. Friends who suspected. I was pregnant couldn't ask because of the previous losses. I wasn't doubting the pregnancy, neither was I fearful. I just wasn't ready, and I was glad we made that decision because the following weeks had an interesting twist.

I started spotting 2 weeks into the pregnancy. I went to the ER and was told it was another ectopic pregnancy. This time, since it was in the right tube - the only remaining fallopian tube, they wanted to operate which meant ending the pregnancy. I was confused and was about to lose my mind, and I stuck out my finger and said, "Devil, not this time." I refused that report and called my doctor from the hospital. He told me not to do the surgery but to come see him the next day. The doctor at the ER wasn't happy with my decision. I was advised to sign documents that I am declining medical treatment. I did that because the doctor treating me at the time told me not to do the surgery.

We went to see my doctor the next day. I was still bleeding that morning when we arrived at his office. The ultrasound indicated no sac in my womb. He said if I'm miscarrying, then nothing can be done to stop it. He asked me to come back a week later.

We left the hospital and went straight to the altar of grace. Prayer changes everything, so that's what we did. However, my husband and I decided to fast and pray. We came into agreement, believing God for a good report, when we went back to see the doctor. No one knew about this, but we stood on this scripture-'When two come into agreement and ask me anything, I will do it.... Matthew 18:19. We were in agreement and believed God would help us (the power of two).

Our one week of waiting to go back for our next doctor's appointment was up. We knew we had done our part by going down on our knees to pray for God to intervene and now believing Him to do His part by saving the situation for the best outcome.

We arrived at the doctor's office with high expectations. We were overwhelmed with joy when the ultrasound revealed it wasn't an ectopic pregnancy, and that everything was fine. What a miracle! Everything looked great, as confirmed by my doctor. The weeks and months that followed were also eventful. This was another high-risk pregnancy, so lots of testing, ultrasounds, and stress tests were done on me.

Everything was going well, with normal pregnancy phases until my doctor's appointment during my 33rd week. That day, I failed the nonstress test, and there was a sign of distress, so additional testing was required. The team of doctors was now talking about early delivery if the baby's condition didn't improve. I was given steroid shots for the speedy development of the baby's lungs. I told myself that she was too small to come now, then I thought it was better that way. Again, I prayed and called our church prayer line for prayers to be said for me. I had my tv on the Christian channel Trinity

Broadcast Network (TBN) as I continually prayed for God to intervene in my situation.

By now, we had spent 2 days, and on day 3, I was told if by noon my situation didn't improve, then I would need to have an emergency C-section. At this point, I thought to myself at this time, it's probably better to deliver today than lose her like my second baby.

That morning, I was watching TBN when Dr. Mike Murdock came on and asked for a $58 seed offering if you're believing God for a miracle. I quickly grabbed my purse and sowed my seed. I say this to the glory of God that before noon, my nurse came and informed me I would be discharged because everything looked great.

Sometimes after a miracle like this, the human mind tries to justify the result and tries to rationalize sense out of it. Still, God deserves all the glory and acknowledgment for such a miraculous turn-around of events for the better. This miracle brought us 3 weeks, good enough to help the baby develop a bit more. My doctor scheduled her birth at 36 weeks, which was 4 weeks earlier than the original due date of August 8th, 2006. He didn't want to take any chances due to my history in childbirth and the new developments of the current pregnancy, and we couldn't agree more. The date was set for the 1st week of July. I packed my stuff and we made it to the hospital by 9am in the morning. My girlfriend also accompanied us to offer her support. Moments before the surgery, I had a panic attack. This was because I kept experiencing flashbacks of the stillbirth, to the point that I couldn't go through the whole process and had to be given general anesthesia.

I didn't see anything; I woke up in pain and my husband who was supposed to be with me during the delivery was not allowed in the delivery room. I was told that things got complications in the delivery room so it was deemed necessary for him to be excused from the delivery room. From what he described, doctors from all over were rushing into my room. He said it was utterly chaotic and nerve-wracking.

Finally, my beautiful baby girl was delivered safely but with underdeveloped lungs, so she was sent to the Neonatal Intensive Care Unit (NICU) and quickly placed in the care of the amazing Ohio State University (OSU) NICU team. My husband went to see her in the incubator, where she was on feeding tubes, but could only see her briefly.

When I woke up from the anesthesia, I was told of the successful delivery of my baby girl. Thank God for my moment of redemption. I have finally delivered my Rainbow baby. The term rainbow baby is used after a parent have had pregnancy losses and finally have a successful delivery. Indeed, God had been good to us. I couldn't go down to see the baby because of the surgery right away. However, that evening, I managed to go down to see her and pump some breast milk for her. The team of nurses in the OSU NICU were amazing. I think it takes special people to do what they do for these babies placed in their care. To me, they're like human angels sent by God to help these vulnerable babies by giving them hope and a chance to live.

In the first 2 days, we weren't allowed to take her out of the incubator, but on the third day, they took her out, and I held her for the first time and breastfed her. She was very tiny but also one of the biggest babies in the NICU. I will go to the NICU in the morning and evenings to feed and cuddle her. Each time I would go down to the NICU, I would sit in awe because no mother would expect to have their baby in the NICU, and for me, it humbled me. I had the utmost respect NICU nurses in the NICU and trusted them to take care of my baby while I was away to get my rest in the afternoons.

On the 4th day after delivery, baby was taken off her breathing tube, so we were hoping to take her home with her, but the doctor said she wasn't ready to go home yet. I was discharged on fifth day, so my husband and I went to the NICU and had our car seat tested and other evaluations for the baby. We were still told that she wasn't ready. Since we couldn't go home with her right of way, we left in the afternoon with hopes of coming back in the evening to visit.

On our drive home, I couldn't stop thinking of her being left at the hospital; a lot went through my mind. I didn't know what I would tell my six-year-old son why his sister couldn't come home with us. We were about 5 minutes from home when my phone rang, and it was the hospital with the nurse on the line. After we left, the doctor came and evaluated her and said she was good to go home. Wow, another miracle! We were both excited and quickly made a U-turn and drove back to get her.

My son came home from school to see his lovely sister, and his eyes were lit up with such excitement. He would help in every way that you could possibly imagine. I couldn't go up and down the stairs due to the surgery, so he would bring me diapers and run miniature errands for me around the house.

After previous losses of my would-be children in my second and third pregnancies came my moment of redemption with the birth of my Rainbow baby. We were beyond grateful and thankful to God for the gift of our daughter.

My son was so happy as he had wished for years for a sibling. Our new addition brought me and my family so much joy and excitement beyond our wildest imagination. This newfound joy and hope gave us a deeper growth in our faith in God. They gave us a sense of purpose, knowing that we would do our best to raise these 2 lovely children under our belt with all the love and care they needed.

Throughout this ordeal, I didn't take a break from school or work. I would always return to work and school right after my eight weeks of healing. I was able to finish my degree, which I was pursuing during my back-to-back losses. Later down the road, I got my MBA.

It wasn't easy getting back and moving on with school and work, but I realized that it helped me to heal. My co-workers were surprised that I didn't take time off. Everyone heals differently. I cried every day for as long as I can remember, even when I returned to work. I realized that staying in mourning is a slippery slope and may lead to depression. Having my son around also helped a great deal. He gave me a sense of purpose and a good reason to live. You can't understand the pain and emotional turmoil that comes with child loss until you experience it. It doesn't help when friends and family come around don't want you to talk about it like it's that easy to get over it. Just because a child wasn't born for everyone to see and interact with doesn't mean their death shouldn't be talked about. The mother grieves in silence because no one has the opportunity to relate to that child. For starters, we went through body changes, and if you were further along like mine, you felt the kicks, the sleepless nights trying to find the right position to sleep. A mother has so many connections with the unborn, not to mention the umbilical cord. Although I had a good support system, but every now and then, I would get one friend or family member who would make insensitive comments and think it was time to get over it. No one purposefully wants to dwell on the death of a child, but you naturally get flashbacks. It's been twenty-one years since my first loss, and I still mourn her death every now and then. I wonder about the role they would have played now; how old they would have been.... etc.

CHAPTER 11

THE ENSUING YEARS AND MY QUEST TO FIND ATIRA

I am very grateful to God for being with me throughout this journey. One may wonder why I am thankful even though I went through turmoil, it's because He preserved the pot. You see, as long as the pot is not broken, its uses are many. I am the pot, and God is the potter (Isaiah 45:9). who am I to say why did God allow this to happen to me. He never forsakes us and is always seeking us out. I had this burning desire that caused me unrest to find closure for Atira. We bonded with her at the hospital, but after the post-mortem, she was brought back to the hospital, and we ordered the hospital to bury her. Later, we received the autopsy report that disclosed hyper coiling of the umbilical cord; I had never heard of it in my life, but that was the cause of death. At this point, the thought of not knowing where Atira was buried was eating me up, so I decided to go on a quest to find out where she was buried. I made numerous calls to the hospital where I delivered her. All attempts to locate my girl failed. We're talking twelve years after her death. I never gave up as I tried calling every week to see if I would get someone who would go the extra mile to help find where my daughter was buried.

One summer morning in 2014, I had an urge to call the hospital again, which I did. That call marked the breakthrough I had been praying for, I was transferred to the chaplain's office. The chaplain on duty was so moved by my story that he promised he would do everything he could to help me find where my baby was taken to and buried. He took my name and number and promised to get back to me. This little light at the end of the tunnel was all I needed. It's just like when Elijah's servant saw a cloud the size of a man's fist (1 Kings 18:44) after he had been checking about seven times for a sign of rain after a long period of drought and famine. In this case, the cloud was a sign of hope that the rains were coming in and the drought and famine were ending. The chaplain offered me a sense of hope as I waited anxiously and believed he would find my daughter's information.

The days that followed were a mixture of excitement and anxiety. Those days felt like weeks, and then the awaited phone call came through. I remember that call like it was yesterday. The chaplain said, and I quote, "We found your baby girl. She was taken to Cooks & Sons funeral home; here is their phone number. You can call them, and they will tell you where your daughter was buried".

I was in awe! I wished he could see how my face was gleaming with excitement and how I would have loved to thank him with a big hug.

I called Cooks & Sons right away. With some research, they confirmed that my baby girl was brought to them, and that they buried her at Obetz

Cemetery. This brought tears to my eyes because the cemetery was about a twenty-minute drive from my house. To to think that my daughter had been this close all this time without my knowledge was very emotional for me.

It was after 4pm when I finally spoke to Joe at Obetz cemetery. He advised me to come the next day. Words can't describe how I felt that day. I was overwhelmed with joy as I told my husband and called friends and family about this great news. Joe had already researched and found the book containing my daughter's information. It was a huge book with tiny handwritten information, so it felt like looking for a needle in a haystack. Joe meticulously and patiently went through the records, looking for Cooks & Sons entries for the year 2002. It took about an hour, and he finally found the plot and took me over to show me the burial site.

My search had finally come to a happy ending. I can't describe the overwhelming peace and gratitude that came over me at that very moment. At long last.... I finally received the closure that I needed! Wow! I had no clue that not only did I I need this to relieve me of the pain of losing Atira and receive a complete healing; especially after being told that the hospital started a common burial for infants right after my loss. I asked Joe if I could build a memorial stone at Atira's burial site, and he sharply said no because the plot was owned by Cooks & Son's funeral home.

After coming to a place of peace and acceptance of the loss of Atira at this point, the family and I made it a standing tradition to take flowers and lay them on her grave on October 21st (Atira's supposed birthday) of each year and anytime we had the opportunity.

CHAPTER

12

Big Breakthrough for Atira

Each time I visited Atira's grave, I wished I had something on it as a memorial. I kept calling Cooks & Sons Funeral Home and Obetz Cemetery so very often to see if their decision had changed but I always received 'no' for an answer.

Two years after discovering Atira's burial site, I had the urge to try and call Obetz Cemetery one last time. I spoke to Joe, who promised to call me back. He called back with the most exciting news ever! He said, it's been fourteen years and I think it will be fine if you put something on the ground for her memorial. I got off the phone and started dancing and rejoicing. I asked my 2 kids what they thought about the memorial, and my son said he thought it was a great idea.

I soon found out that tombstones weren't cheap. However, the God of possibilities, however, led me to the Columbus Art Memorial. The owner heard my story, gave me a good price, and started working with Obetz

Cemetery to get permission to install the tombstone and memorial. I wanted her picture on the tombstone and was advised that pictures are done abroad and could take you 3 months to get the picture back. Working with the cemetery to approve the memorial stone also took some time. I thought it was going to be easy and quick, There was this concrete pouring process, which takes time, not to mention the backlog of other people already in line ahead me.

Finally in 2017, right before Atira's supposed birthday, the memorial was installed. Wishes fulfilled, we now had a memorial stone for Atira. Praise God! This is so true in my situation according to the Book of Matthew 7:7-8, which says, 'Ask, and it shall be given you; seek, and you shall find; knock, and it shall be opened unto you.

CHAPTER 13

COUNTING ON WITH GRATITUDE

Life Reflection

Embracing life after facing profound loss and despair transformed me in ways I could never have imagined. Rather than breaking me, the heartbreak and grief acted as a crucible, forging a version of myself that was more resilient, empathetic, and determined than ever before. These trials and my formal education gave me a unique perspective on life that I felt compelled to share with others.

When I took on a role in a Fortune 500 Company, it wasn't just a job but a platform. The position in the corporate world brought with it an intricate web of responsibilities and opportunities. The experience honed my skills and imbued me with a fresh outlook on problem-solving, leadership, and mentoring.

It wasn't just about corporate success. Deep down inside. I felt a calling to help others rediscover their purpose and zest for life. That's how I began my journey as a life coach. Despite their brave fronts, I realized that many around us battle inner terrors, traumas, or simply, a loss of direction. And if I, after my personal tragedies, could find a path forward, so could they— with a little guidance.

I worked with individuals and veterans hoping to advance their business prospects and careers.

It's incredibly meaningful to be part of communities that provide comfort and understanding, especially through the trials of infertility and loss. In 'The Grieving Moms' Facebook group, women who have endured the heartache of pregnancy loss and infertility challenges come together. This space offers a sanctuary where members can share their grief openly, find mutual support, and navigate the complex emotions associated with their experiences. The group's purpose is to console and foster resilience and healing among its members.

On the other hand, 'Rainbow Babies' is a group that represents hope and renewal. It consists of women who have experienced the joy of conceiving a child following previous losses — these are their 'rainbow babies,' This name represents the beauty and hope that follows a storm. The group also warmly includes those who are still in anticipation of such joy, providing a community that celebrates triumphs and offers encouragement during the wait.

Both groups not only represent the spectrum of experiences related to fertility struggles — from the depths of sorrow to the heights of joy but they stand as pillars of support, offering a place where women can connect, share their journeys, and find solace in the company of those who truly understand.

I count myself exceedingly blessed that through the tapestry of life's struggles, I've managed to march onward, fortified not by my strength alone, but also by the sustaining grace of a higher power. This journey has been far from solitary. It has been profoundly shaped by the unshakeable pillars of support offered by my dear family and a circle of friends whose encouragement has been as constant as the northern star. As I look back upon the myriad of footsteps that mark my path, it becomes clear that such a voyage would have been a Sisyphean task without the omnipresent support of the Almighty God. In the sanctuary of my soul, I honor the Lord as Elohim, the embodiment of might, and as El Shaddai, the majestic ruler who reigns from the celestial realms.

The possibility that my voice may never echo through vast halls, reaching thousands simultaneously, is tempered by a serene acceptance and a hopeful aspiration. With this book, I aspire to extend my story beyond the confines of spoken words to connect with kindred spirits worldwide, even if just a handful at a time. It is my earnest desire to share a message of resilience and optimism, to offer a beacon of hope that shines with the promise that the miracles witnessed in my life are not mine alone to cherish. For in the eyes of the Divine, no favoritism exists; His benevolent reach extends to all.

Let this narrative not just be a memoir, but a source of solace and inspiration, a reminder that the Divine crafts possibility from the implausible, making ways where paths seem non-existent. May it serve as a testament to the power of faith and as an assurance that if the Divine architect has orchestrated such wonders in my life, then surely, the same boundless potential lies waiting for each soul brave enough to believe. With the Divine as the inexhaustible wellspring of strength, what one heart has overcome, another's can too.

Lessons Learned Along the Way

Can a person with children still have fertility issues after childbirth? Absolutely, I came to learn that you can have childbearing issues even after having children. When that happens, it is okay to seek help. I also learned that not all pregnancies are the same.

My journey through childbirth has been a true blessing, to say the least. I can confidently say that the experiences I went through have helped shaped me into the person I am today - a woman full of faith, tenacity, courage, confidence, and optimism; a woman with a zest for life to help give a voice of reason to others who may have lost hope to achieve a fulfilled and successful life, especially after experiencing some of life's most upsetting moments and events.

I learned that in life, things happen and may not go completely as planned, but our response and choices to unfortunate and terrible events can help us make the most out of our situations if we choose not to concentrate on the negative aspects of our circumstances.

In reflecting on the profound lessons of life, I have arrived at a place of profound gratitude, recognizing that children are indeed treasures to be held dear. The journey to parenthood, however, is not uniform for all. While some may traverse life without any hindrances, others find themselves at a juncture of infertility, feeling as if they stand at a crossroads with no discernible exit.

It's a poignant truth that having one or even two children does not make one immune to experiencing fertility challenges in the future. I, too, have lived this reality. After the joy and tribulation of four pregnancies, from which I was blessed with two wonderful children, my own ability to conceive seemed to be put on pause and remained unchanged since 2005. To those who long to hear the pitter-patter of little feet, yet still find it beyond their reach, please know that it is perfectly acceptable to seek guidance and assistance.

I recall the day I reached out to a respected elder from my church, after wrestling with whether seeking fertility treatment aligned with my faith and values. The fear that such actions might be perceived as stepping outside the bounds of what was acceptable weighed heavily on me. His assurance that pursuing medical help was acceptable and advisable was a balm to my anxious heart.

Education became my ally in this journey. I delved into the complexities of fibroids and the intricacies of fertility treatments. Facing my deep-seated aversion to needles, the prospect of self-administering injections was daunting. I doubted my strength to overcome this hurdle.

This story is shared not just as a personal chronicle but as an outreach to others who might see their own struggles mirrored in mine. It is a call to action, a gentle nudge to embrace the support systems around you, to seek knowledge, and to find solace in the shared experiences of others. The road to parenthood, with its unpredictability, is a testament to the resilience of the human spirit and the boundless capacity for hope.

The journey of a couple grappling with infertility and the profound sorrow that accompanies the loss of a child is a deeply personal and often isolating experience. The silence surrounding these issues can be deafening, and their challenges are immense, stretching the emotional and sometimes the physical bonds of a marriage to it's limits. In such moments, the weight of despair and hopelessness can be overwhelming, leading many couples to contemplate the dissolution of their marriage as they struggle to cope with the pain and disappointment.

However, within this crucible of suffering, I extend a message of hope—a plea for those enduring such trials to cling steadfastly to one another and their shared dreams of having a family. This encouragement springs from a well of personal hardship and eventual triumph, a testament to the belief that, in the presence of faith, even the most daunting circumstances can yield to perseverance and grace.

My story is not unique, but it is one steeped in the conviction that a higher power is at play beyond our limited reserves of strength. Through the darkest times, when all seemed lost, I discovered reservoirs of resilience and courage bestowed by a benevolent force—a strength I attribute to the divine. This is a strength that lies dormant within each of us, waiting to be summoned in times of crisis.

When we find ourselves at the edge of despair, when every setback chips away at our resolve, it is crucial to remember that we are not alone. In these moments of trial, we must reach deep within and draw upon the inner strength that God has imbued within in us. It is a strength that enables us to bear the unbearable, to hope against hope, and to emerge from tribulation with a renewed spirit and a stronger bond.

I share these reflections as a beacon of hope for those navigating through the turbulence of loss and the unfulfilled yearning for a child. May my life and my journey serve as a reminder of the immense potential for transformation and healing. It is through tapping into our divine inner strength that we can face our darkest hours with courage and emerge with a renewed commitment to each other and to the shared vision of a family we hold dear.

May this knowledge serve as a wellspring of determination for all those who find themselves in the throes of such profound challenges. May they be encouraged to persevere for a future where love and unity forge a path towards finding a fulfilling and flourishing marriage and family life.

My journey through life has unfolded in a way that has brought me back to the beginning, yet with a richer sense of thankfulness than I ever could have anticipated. There's been an awakening within me, an eye-opening realization that my path is nothing short of miraculous. Each twist and turn and every high and low, has contributed to a larger tapestry that I can now step back and appreciate in its entirety. The notion that these diverse experiences were intricately designed to shape me for the better is a perspective I've found reflected in the wisdom of Romans 8:28.

This epiphany has been transformative. It's as if reaching this place of inner peace and profound gratitude has unlocked a wellspring of confidence within me. The silence I once maintained, the stories I kept shrouded in the shadows of nervousness and hesitation, I now feel empowered to bring into the light. The reticence has been replaced with a readiness to speak my truth, and to share the narrative of my past with any open heart.

In sharing my experiences, I've discovered a powerful sense of liberation. It's as though in talking about my journey, I'm not just recounting events but also connecting dots that outline the growth and resilience that were quietly taking shape all along. It is an invitation to others to find solace in their own stories, to recognize that their struggles and triumphs are not solitary incidents, but part of a grander design that can lead to personal growth and collective empathy.

Indeed, the journey to this moment has been intricate and, at times, arduous. But the realization that everything I've endured was shaping me into who I am today has allowed me to embrace my history with a sense of purpose and look forward to the future with hope. The vulnerability that once held me back now propels me forward, encouraging me to engage with the world in a cathartic way and hopefully inspiring for other along the journey,

THERE WILL ALWAYS BE A GENESIS AND A REVELATION.

Every challenge you face is more than a mere obstacle; it is part of a grander narrative that traces back to a beginning—a "Genesis"—where the seeds of your current circumstances were planted. By looking back to the past and understanding where your path commenced, you can reconstruct your journey through times of hardship. It is within this introspection that you'll discover the roots of your struggles and the strength you've gained along the way.

If you are currently facing the dawn of a challenging period, your "Genesis," I urge you to grasp tightly to your resilience and faith. Trust in the process because the unfolding of your story is leading towards an enlightening culmination—a "Revelation." This revelation is a promise of hope and fulfillment. It could manifest as the laughter of a child you've been yearning for, the satisfaction of landing your ideal job, or witnessing a long-awaited positive transformation in a family member. These are not just fanciful dreams; they are potential chapters of your life that await you.

The journey from "Genesis" to "Revelation" is not a straight path. It is an intricate tapestry of many chapters. Just like the pages of a book, some will turn with ease and joy, while others may find it difficult to get through, due to facing many trials and tribulations. These challenging chapters, however uncomfortable they may be, are integral to your growth. They add depth and complexity to your story, while providing context and contrast to the joyous triumphs that lie ahead.

God's handiwork is evident in the narrative of your life, with every chapter meticulously crafted for a purpose. No detail is superfluous in His storytelling, and no moment is without meaning. This divine craftsmanship ensures the value of each experience you encounter.

Amidst it all, faith is the anchor that will sustain you. It is the most cherished possession That will carry you forward, bridging the gap between your "Genesis" and your "Revelation." This faith doesn't need to be monumental to be effective; even faith, as minuscule as a mustard seed, has the power to move mountains. This persistent, unwavering belief will keep the pages turning, guiding you through every chapter until the story reaches its destined conclusion. So, embrace your faith, nurture it, and let it guide you through the narrative of your life toward the revelation of your deepest aspirations and the realization of your purpose.

> For truly I tell you, if you have faith the size of a mustard seed, you will say to this mountain, 'Move from here to there,' and it will move, and nothing will be impossible for you.
> (Matthew 17:20-21) "

ABOUT THE AUTHOR

Dotty is a dedicated and certified life career coach, as well as the founder of Dorothy Coaching Services. In this book, she has decided to share her own experiences, knowing it's the right time to pour her heart out to her readers. This decision is driven by her belief that through sharing our personal stories, we can bring solace to those in similar situations and even help them see a way forward.

Dorothy is certain that her story may not resonate with everyone, but she is compelled to share it, knowing that there is someone out there who needs to hear it. In this book, she invites you to journey through her life—an incredible and impactful journey that has been a blessing in disguise. The narrative is filled with highs, lows, and "face palming" moments, showing how her life was shaped and how she managed to rise above the challenges she encountered.

She acknowledges that without divine intervention, none of her achievements would have been possible. Her faith has served as her cornerstone, guiding her through life's maze and helping her attain her current position.

Dorothy is married and a proud mother of two wonderful children. Through her work, she has had the privilege to interact with people from diverse backgrounds, assisting them in finding hope and encouragement. Her ultimate goal is to guide as many people as possible toward leading fulfilled and successful lives.

Through this book, Dorothy aims to inspire, motivate, and touch lives by using her own experiences as a tool. She is a living testament to the fact that one can turn their stumbling blocks into steppingstones, and she passionately believes in sharing that knowledge with others.

For I know the plans I have for you," declares the Lord, "plans to prosper you and not to harm you, plans to give you hope and a future.
Jeremiah 29:11

Below is the letter of advice would have given myself 24 years ago to help prepare and encourage me for what I was about to go through.

November 30th 1999

Dear Dorothy

I hope this letter finds you in good health and spirits, despite the challenging times you may be facing. Today, I want to reach out to you with a message of strength, resilience, and hope. Life, in its unpredictable journey, often brings us to crossroads of adversity and trials. It is in these moments, however, that your strength is truly tested and your resilience is forged.

I understand that facing adversity is never easy. It can be a daunting and often lonely path. You might feel overwhelmed, scared, or even lost. But remember, it is during these times that our character is shaped and our inner strength is built. Each challenge you overcome is a testament to your courage and determination.

I urge you to hold on to hope, even when it seems like a faint glimmer in the darkness. Hope has the power to light your path and guide you through the toughest of times. It is the anchor that keeps us grounded when the storms of life rage around us. Remember, after every storm, there comes a calm. Your present struggles are not your destination, they are merely steppingstones to a stronger and more resilient you.

Lean on the support of family, friends, and your community. No one is meant to face life's trials alone. The comfort and understanding of loved ones can be a powerful source of strength. Moreover, do not hesitate to seek out stories of others who have faced similar challenges. Their journeys of overcoming adversity can offer you inspiration and practical insights.

Most importantly, be kind to yourself. Recognize your efforts, celebrate your small victories, and forgive yourself for any setbacks. Personal growth is a journey, not a race. Celebrate each step, no matter how small the progress.

As am writing to you, I am reminded of the resilience and strength that lies within you. Your journey, with all its ups and downs, is a powerful narrative of human perseverance. I believe in your ability to rise above the challenges and emerge stronger and wiser.

Stay strong, keep fighting, and hold on to hope. You have within you all the strength and courage you need to conquer the adversities you face.

Remember, you are not alone in this journey, you have the all-powerful, all-knowing, El Shaddai, Elohim……the ancient of days on your side.

With heartfelt encouragement and unwavering support.

Love Dorothy

Dorothy, shares personal anecdotes and practical insights, unveiling the significance of hope in shaping destinies and navigating uncertainties. Through empowering exercises and real-life examples, readers are encouraged to awaken hope's dormant energies within, unlocking a reservoir of strength, resilience, and unwavering optimism.

*Evg. Clarence C. Serebour | (President, CCWorldEvangelism)

Dorothy, a virtuous, strong, selfless, God-fearing woman of noble character. A proverb 31 woman indeed, for she doth rise early, considers a field and buyeth it. Dorothy is an ambitious, motivated go-getter she epitomizes the meaning of a virtuous woman. She is a living testament of the manifestation of the Lord's presence in someone's life. Well done and congratulations my dear friend and sister.

Leah Porter | IT Project Manager

This book is a poignant portrayal of Dorothy's personal story of going from tragedy to triumph. She takes us behind the scenes to look at her private struggles and relentless pursuit to fulfill a life-long dream in the midst of incredible challenges. This story is also a testimony of how when you submit your life to God and allow Him to help you navigate during your tough times, He will empower you with courage to conquer every fear and doubt, and strengthen you to overcome every test and trial. Through her remarkable journey of faith, Dorothy releases her crushed dreams that eventually become the ashes that fertilize beautiful new beginnings where her hope is renewed to rise again.

Shanda Harris | Small Business Advocate

Made in the USA
Coppell, TX
12 January 2024